Management

Guide for First-Time Manager, Effective Strategies to Improve Leadership and Management Skills with 10 Management Models

By:

James Stevens

Published by Shepal Publishing Co.
All Rights Reserved
Copyright 2016, New York

Table of Contents

Introduction

Being a manager can be a challenge, especially if you do not have the right experience to determine whether you are doing the right thing or now. That is why you need to have strategies from management experts at your fingertips, so that you can reflect on some sound advice that will help you to further your ability to manage people and your workplace.

This book contains strategies that have been derived from management models. As first time managers will face an array of difficult situations, the models are all different and designed to help you through every situation.

For ease of understanding, they have been explained in groups, based on their relevance to the process of improving management and leaderships skills.

This book is meant to be a tool that will guide you through the entire process of being a first time manager. Through it, you will learn what you need to do to cope when things become challenging, and how you can elevate your workplace with your efforts. Read through each strategy and you will find ways that you can apply them for success. Use this book to become the best manager that you can be, so that you can continue to risk up the ranks of your organisation.

Chapter 1:
What Being a Leader
and a Manager is all About

Heading a large organisation with a substantial amount of staff obediently following instructions can sound like a dream come true. This has even more meaning when all these employees are working towards fulfilling a dream of achieving profitability, and doing a good job of it as well. The organisations that have managed to achieve this have one thing in common, exceptional leadership and professional management.

This sounds intimidating, but it really is not. It is all about understanding what would be expected from you as a leader or manager in an organisation, and how you can get the best results. If you have finally worked your way to the top from a supervisory position into management, congratulations. Perhaps you have finalised your college degree and are working at your first management job. Whatever journey you have taken does not matter too much at this point, as you are about to embark on another one, and that is to be a manager for the first time.

Managers are expected to know everything about the business, and they have to be able to control the staff, control the business, control the customer and control themselves. It is a lot to take on, and often, things seem to fall through the cracks. However, it is possible to develop management skills so that this entire process moves smoothly. Before that, it is essential to differentiate between a leader and a manager.

Leaders and Managers

These terms are often used together though they have differing meanings. Leaders are people that others follow. They are the ones whose actions you will try to emulate, who you look to for direction and inspiration when you are feeling lost or confused in the workplace. Leaders are friendly and approachable. A manager on the other hand, is someone that you work for. Where the leader is your inspiring friend, the manager is your boss. When a manager gives an instruction, you follow it, when they have a demand, you ensure that it has been fulfilled. A manager is the person who makes responsible decisions and who takes the blame for the team when things go wrong.

Any manager who is looking to be successful needs to have the right management skills in order to succeed. However, there also needs to be some element of leadership within these so that the employee is able to take and follow instructions, as well as to connect with the person that is giving the instructions. Now you need to understand what these management skills and leadership skills are.

Management Skills

As a new manager, you may feel as though you are lost at sea when faced with managing people for the first time. There are five skills that will help you to get started so that you can cope with any situation that is brought upon you as a manager.

The first of these is human resource management, as you will become the sounding board for a host of issues related to employees and their relationships with each other and the company. You need to be able to deal with these issues so that your staff are able to work as a team and meet the objectives of the organisation.

Next, you have to be able to motivate the employees you are responsible for. If they are passionate about their work, they will always be on time, complete the tasks that are assigned and maintain a positive attitude. If they are not, you will spend a considerable amount of your time trouble shooting and trying to resolve issues all the time,

The third skill that you need is ensuring that you always have the resources that you need to get the job done. Running out of things slows down work and will reveal that you are inefficient. You have to stay on top of this as your decisions will affect every single person that you are managing.

Fourth, you must be objective enough to make accurate performance reviews for your staff. This may mean that you give a negative review to someone that you like, but the bottom line is business must go on, and you have to make decisions that put business first.

Finally, your team should know that you have a plan and direction for them so you should create a clear career path. Following this path will mean that there are opportunities for growth, promotion, increased compensation and a better future. This needs to be clear to your staff, as it can affect their overall productivity.

Leadership Skills

Leaders are different from managers as has been established so far. As a first time manager, you can benefit from having three leadership skills. The first one is communication, which is the ability to speak to your staff and have them understand your message in the right way. A good leader will have nothing lost in translation and will ensure that anything they attempted to communicate is clear, so that any resulting actions are clear as well.

Next, you need to be organised. Know what you have to do, the order that you will start and complete a task and be clear about who is responsible. Organisation will ensure that you do not get overwhelmed with work or your new found responsibility.

Finally, you must be confident and believe in what you have to say and the decisions that you need to make. This will give others the passion that they need to believe in you and your ideals. Confidence can carry you forward in any situation, even when you may be wrong.

With this as your foundation, you are ready to embark on the journey of a first time manager. Nonetheless, you need to realise that you are not the first person to walk this part and there have been dozens before you. Looking back at history, you will find that people in management have been coming up with theories to help managers become better at what they do. These have turned into strategies which are designed to ensure you get all that you need as a manager, by the way that you behave and treat your subordinates. Rather than reinvent the wheel, the next chapters contain ten of the most popular management models. You will find in one of them all that you need to succeed as a first time manager.

Chapter 2:
How to Improve Your Management and Leadership Skills

Leadership is not just about holding a high position and being in charge of a certain team; there is more to leadership than this. It is also not about telling your team what to do at all times. A manager and a leader have a lot more to do, that is why it is important to know how you can improve your leadership skills to become a better leader to the team that you are leading all the time. If you are an ineffective leader, your team will never take you seriously and you will not be able to guide them or even to motivate them to accomplish the goals that you have already set. This is the reason why you need these simple but very effective tips to help you improve on the management and leadership skills that you already have to become a better leader even to the team that you are leading:

a) Communicate and stay connected

Leadership and management calls for some degree of trust and understanding between the team that you are leading and the leader/manager. For this to be achieved, the manager should learn how to connect to his team in a manner that they will feel safe and free around him. This is the only way they will trust him to confide in him and to follow his instructions without questioning. So many factors will come into play here in order for a leader to receive total trust from the team that he is leading. Some of the traits that will help a leader achieve this are positivity, empathy, purposefulness, compassionate, humble and loving. These traits will genuinely connect you to your team and bring you closer to them.

The reason why this is important is because a close connection to the people you are leading generates trust among yourselves and this is what helps in building a strong relationship and a culture that will help each of them become accountable and exceptional in performance. This will in the end translate to a successful project.

b) Encourage creative thinking and skills

Creative thinking is what brings about brainstorming and exploration and this is what will help your team to work better. You therefore need to allow creativity in your team if you want to achieve the best results ever. As a good leader, you should be open to opinions and ideas coming from your team. You should be able to accept some of their suggestions if not all of them and put them into action. You should also give them some challenges to trigger their creativity, this will kill boredom and also bring out the best in them. This also works to boost their confidence in their abilities and your trust in them.

c) Get to know your team better

With the connection established above and good communication, knowing your team better will be very easy. The things that should interest you so much in your team are exactly who they are, what their interests are and the talent that they possess, which can help in the project that you are handling. Many managers do not take time to learn about the people in their team. They concentrate on the mission and vision, without realising that knowing your own people is equally important in management. When you know more about your people, you can show concern and even take care of them better. This will make it easy for them to take care of your customers better and achieving your goal will much easier. Therefore, as a good leader you have to be the one that knows your team better than anyone else. You should be able to tell each of their strong skills, their weaknesses and how they can be utilized in the business.

d) Lead by example

Many managers issue out instructions all day and by the end of the day, they are not happy with the way things were done. A good leader will not just tell what needs to be done; he will show how it should be done. You should know how to show your team what they should know and not just tell them what to do. Telling people what to do is not always well received and people might see you as a dictator but working with your team will give them the motivation to work for the results that you are anticipating. They will even go an extra mile just to please you.

e) Emphasize on the positive things

Leadership is not as simple as it sounds. Challenges are all over and a leader will face many difficulties with his team. The way he reacts to these difficulties or problems will determine his success as a leader. Since it will be hard to enjoy a smooth ride as a leader, purpose to only focus on the positive things and not on the negative issues that can bring down your team in just seconds. Sometimes this will not be easy, especially if a major error occurs and it is costing the business a lot of money. That is why a manager should be an exceptional person, who is able to handle all situations in calmness without letting anger and frustration get in his way. Always be the one seeking for a positive thing in a situation however bad it is and you will succeed in leadership. You should realize that the more you see a positive aspect in an issue, the more ideas flow through your mind and the issue can be fixed on time.

f) Know what motivates you

Always know that your team will be watching you closely and they will be enthusiastic to work if you are also up to the task. That is why it is good to know what motivates you so that you will be motivated at all times. If you are a leader that only sees your role as just a job, you will definitely show it to your team and they may start taking their roles and responsibilities as just a job. Good results cannot be achieved this way. If on the other hand you want to inspire people to do their best in life, your team will see it and they will work with you on that.

Chapter 3:
The Hierarchy, the Five Forces and the Situation

There are famous management gurus who have created models for management that are as applicable today as they were when they were first being drafted decades ago. In this section, improving your management skills will be evaluated from three models. These are Maslow's Hierarchy of Needs, Porter's Five Competitive Forces and Hershey's Situational Leadership.

Maslow's Hierarchy of Needs

In order to inspire a team of people, a manager needs to be able to determine what motivates the members of that team, and Maslow's hierarchy of needs provides information that explains that. It has a pyramid shaped diagram that contains five levels, each level representing a type of need.

The best way to ensure that staff are motivated is to show them that as a manager, you can help the move from one way to another. At the base if the pyramid are the physiological needs, which are related to what we need to survive. These include the need for food and water and even sleep. The next level is safety needs, which is concerned with our overall stability in the world. These can affect our psychological state. In the work place, they would include a sense of belonging, which makes one enjoy feelings of safety and as though they are a part of the group.

From this, it is possible to move to the next level which is about love and being a team member. At this stage, in addition to belonging to a group, an employee may also want to feel appreciated as a member of staff. These is a need to feel important and as though the employee makes a contribution to business success. As a manager, you must develop your human resource management skills so that you can create this feeling and unity.

The fourth level is the need for self-esteem. This happens when your team reach the level of promotion, and they are receiving attention and recognition from other people for the efforts they have put in and what they have accomplished. They will not be interested in having some power, and as the manager, you would be tasked with giving them more responsibility.

The final level is the self-actualisation level, and this is one that people will reach when they have attained the highest position of management that is available. When you attain this level, you have maximised all of your attention and have nothing left to give. Now you are able to freely look for more knowledge and spiritual enlightenment.

Porter's Five Competitive Forces

Strategic thinking comes to life with Porter's Five Competitive Forces model, and in order to succeed as a manager, you need to be able to strategize on ways that you can improve your business in the future. The first part of this model looks at competitors and gets the manager to address how many of them exist, and what advantage they have within the market. It also helps the manager evaluate their position, so that they can determine whether they are strong enough to withstand the competition.

When the manager understands the stakes in this regard, it becomes possible to improve the skill of provision of resources so that business operations can continue smoothly.

The second competitive force is the threat of substitution where the manager evaluates whether it is possible that the competition can create a cheaper product that delivers the same customer satisfaction. This would lead the manager to evaluate existing processes and determine the way that they contribute to overall productivity.

This is followed by bargaining power over the customers. If the customer consistently wants to use the product, does the company have enough power to ensure that they are able to continue selling in large volumes. This is followed by bargaining power of the suppliers, so as to understand what would happen to the business in case of a change if supplied. Would it stop functioning at optimum levels or would a change in the supplier's prices force the organisation to change their prices as well. It is good to establish a strong relationship with a supplier, but it is not recommended that the supplier be given too much power.

The final competitive force is rivalry among the existing players. This is where the manager looks at the competitive advantage, to determine how much better it is in the market. In order to stand out and motivate the employees to meet a goal, they need to realise that the goal they are working for is attainable and unique. They have to believe that they are working for a winning organisation.

These five forces help a manager to evaluate what is happening in the environment outside of the organisation, so that they can make decisions that will help improve the organisation from within.

Hersey's and Blanchard's Situational Leadership

With this model, the focus for the manager is on being flexible and adaptable to any situation that they may face. It is understood that not all leadership styles are the same, and there needs to be some allowance in the way that leadership styles are applied to a situation.

In situational leadership, there are four main behaviours that a manager needs to consider. There are telling, selling, participating and delegating. With telling, it means that there are times that the leader needs to take an authoritative stance and give directions that everyone else is meant to follow. Selling requires the manager to be more persuasive and to convince the people that are being managed to take a certain action. Then, there is participating where the leader is tasked with taking into consideration the opinions of people within a group and operating like a democracy. Finally, with delegating, it is sharing responsibility, so that the manager is able to monitor what is happening without having to become too involved.

Managers must be mutable for success, and able to adapt to all these situations with ease. This theory is one that is consistently applied in various degrees in almost all organisations.

Chapter 4:
Change and Innovation

The next three management models deal with change and innovation in management. It is said that the one thing that remains permanent in an organisation is change. Therefore, as a manager, you need to be able to manage change in such a way that it is not disruptive to the company. The three theories that are addressed in this section are Kotter's Change Phases, Beckhard's Change Equation and Christensen's Disruptive Innovation.

Kotter Change Phases

As a new first time manager, you will have bit ideas of how you can improve the department that you are working in, and that often requires you to implement some change. For your change to be successful, you must get everyone on board and that is what Kotter's phases are all about. There are eight phase in total that must be followed one after the other in order for there to be lasting change.

The first phase calls for you to create a sense of urgency. This will motivate people to feel that the change is necessary, and they will become motivated to follow through with this change. As the manager, you need to make your staff feel as though the change resonates from within them, and that they can truly lead it going forward.

After this, you must form a powerful coalition, where you identify the change leaders who are within the company and ensure that they are all on board to implement your plan. Change is more effective when people are working as part of a team, than when there are individuals simple working on their own to make a difference. As manager, you have to be the head of the coalition that you create, so that everyone else sees you as the leader of the change.

To communicate this change, you must create a clear vision that others within the company are able to understand and relate to. This will help other picture the end result of what you are working towards, which should help them to commit to the entire process. Once the vision has been created it must be communicated, and this should be done in a relaxed manner. The key for any manager is to make sure that their communication blends in to the work that is being, so that the change appears to be unobtrusive to their overall work process. This requires the manager to be an example and live the change they are talking about.

The fifth phase deals with the removal of obstacles, and in this instance the obstacles would be anyone that is coming in the way of the change you are working on. Here you should be getting rid of obstacles and by doing so you will empower other people within the company to facilitate the vision and the change.

For them to be motivated to do so, it is necessary to create some short term wins, which are milestones that shall be used to evaluate the process of change. There shall be some reward for each person that is able to meet a change target, as this will help towards motivating everyone within the group.

This will result in you building on the change, and not allowing the transition to be the end of it. A period of continuous improvement will be imminent and shall continue until the change has fully taken root. The last phase that Kotter proposed was to have the change anchored in corporate culture, so that it becomes a part of what is achieved on a daily basis.

Beckhard's Change Equation

In this equation, Beckhard explains what is happening with change by evaluating four main factors. These are dissatisfaction with the present, a vision of the way that things could be, the knowledge of the first steps to be taken and the resistance to change. Resistance to change is at the end of the equation, and will only be manageable if the other three factors are lower in value than the resistance.

This equation highlights something that is quite important, and that is that many efforts to change will fail because people choose to be resistant to change, refusing to allow it to happen naturally.

The manager can use this model as a practical and simple guide to understand what is happening with change in their organisation, though it must be noted that this equation is simple and lacks in dimension. There are many additional attributes that can be considered though for now, these are the ones in the equation. In addition, it becomes challenging to figure out the balance as there is no clear idea as to which of these factors carries the most weight.

Christensen's Disruptive Innovation

This looks at what happens within an organisation when you change the technologies and in this way, disrupt the way that things are done. New technologies take some getting used to and a good manager will ensure that there are systems in place that can handle the changes. The reasons that as a manager you may choose to change the technologies that are used include cutting down on costs so that you can make more profit, or simplifying the way that things are currently being done within the organisation. It is wrong to assume that an entire organisation could collapse simply because it made the move to implement change. Instead, managers need to be able to take control of the situation, so that things do not go out of hand. This requires the manager to develop the skill of strategic thinking, and be able to anticipate everything that could go wrong so that it is dealt with in good time.

Chapter 5:
Objectives, Team Development and Culture

The next three management models are helpful in varying ways to the manager. These models include Drucker's Management of Objectives, Tuckman's Stages of Team Development and Schein's Three Levels of Culture. With these models, the manager is able to deal with motivating the team to reach a certain goal. They require for an understanding of the employees within the whole process, and how the company can accommodate them and their needs for the best results.

Drucker's Management of Objectives

Every company has goals that it is working towards meeting and in order to meet those goals, the employees need to carry out certain tasks in certain ways. To motivate the employees and also to keep them in check, they are given specific objectives that they have to meet. A first time manager will do what is necessary to ensure that the goals of the organisation are aligned with the goals of the employee. That is what management of objectives is all about.

This requires the manager to get organised and to ensure that everyone in the organisation is clear about what their responsibilities are. The manager will also need to be democratic and to take into consideration the opinions and thoughts of the workers in the organisation.

To ensure that the desired results are attained, there will be a time period that is set, and from this, it will be possible to measure milestones. This will then bring forth one of the primary skills that a new manager is supposed to have, and that is the ability to do an evaluation of the performance of the staff.

It is from Drucker that the famous SMART goals were devised. For a manager, going back to SMART when making a decision will help to ensure that the decision is viable and will deliver the expected result. SMART stands for specific, measurable, achievable, realistic and time-related.

Tuckman's Stages of Team Development

When it comes to team work, a first time manager can face a significant challenge. With no experience on how to create and manage a team, the dynamics of dominating personalities, a lack of motivation and no cohesion could make the entire process of team development highly stressful and ineffective. Realising that this could be an issue that affects the productivity of a company, Tuckman devised a process to help a manager create a team.

The first phase of this process is the forming of the team. At this point, a project has already been identified and the initial team is put together. This allows the manager to observe the way that members within the team are interacting with each other before a project is started and underway. From this, it becomes easier for the manager to select the final team members, and for those members to come together and choose a leader. When this happens, the manager knows that they have made a good decision and are on the right track.

The next phase is storming, and this is where members of the team are allowed to share their ideas so that a way forward can be mapped. Without the proper guidance, this stage can become vicious and there could be passionate disagreements that disrupt the process. The manager has delegated the responsibilities of the team to the project manager, who calms everyone down, and gives all the chance to share their opinion. Through consensus, a decision is made.

While the team is figuring out their own identity, they will go through a phase that is known as norming. In this phase, all the rules of engagement and behaviour are established. The team members are supposed to be able to work together, and any authoritative decisions that had been made by the project manager have now become more authoritative. As a first time manager, you should be able to observe what is happening within the team without having to get involved in its operations.

The next step of the process looks at performance. This is evidence for the manager that the team is able to carry out the tasks for which it had been designed. Everyone is actively playing their part to meet the goals of the team and the company as well. The team should be able to motivate itself through the members and be determines to show results. The project manager's role has diminished slightly as the members of the team are able to make their own decisions.

The final step of the team development process is known as adjourning. For the first time manager, the task that the team was created to fulfil has been completed and there is no need to keep the team functional or operational any more. Therefore, this is when the team is dismantled and work goes back to the way it has normally been.

Having this process to follow as a guide helps to make a manager more organised in their work, and also more results oriented. It is easier to plan, and the work load does not fall too heavily on the shoulders of the manager. Once the team has been put together, the first time manager is able to watch from the side-lines as the team develops.

Schein's Three Levels of Culture

This management model seeks to address an issue that can cause considerable frustration to a first time manager and that is organisational culture. When a company is used to operating in a certain manner, carrying out their tasks in a way that is not effective and refusing to change it, the manager is likely dealing with a situation where the excuse given is 'this is the way that it has always been' and this type of excuse is not productive for the organisation.

According to Schein, there are three levels that need to be considered. The first is known as artefacts. At this level, there are things that can be observed on the surface and these are possible the easiest things that one can change within the organisation. These include the way that people dress, the way that the office is arranged and general manner of behaviour. The challenge a manger will face when dealing with these is perspective, as what may be correct for one individual could prove to be wrong or immoral for someone else. This requires some diplomacy and tact to be adequately addressed.

The second level deals with espoused values. These are the values that are within all people, the ones that they are conscious too. Normally, they are ingrained in a person from their childhood, and they remain as firm ideas even after the person has grown up. These are the way that people strategize, and also deals with the philosophies that are to be followed.

The third and final level addresses basic assumptions and values. This is what culture us all about, what it is based on and what happens within us at an unconscious stage. They help us to understand the reason that we behave in a certain way, or why we take certain actions. These in essence deal with what it means to be a human being. A manager who is looking to lead and motivate a team needs to understand these levels of culture so that they are better able to see what people are all about.

Chapter 6:
Leadership Pipeline

This is the final management model that a first time manager should consider, and it deals with the way that managers are selected to go up the ranks in an organisation. If as a manager you have been internally promoted, then it is as a result of the leadership pipeline. This is all about growing an individual in the company, so that they can get to the stage where they grow from lower management and work their way up to the highest levels of management.

Like other management models, this has six stages that one needs to go through. To begin with there is the change from managing oneself to managing a group of other people. This happens when one becomes the leader of a team or project manager. As a first time manager, this is where you begin to rise up the ranks.

The next stage looks at moving from managing other people to managing managers. From here, the manger then manages functional managers, moving to business managers, then to group managers and finally to enterprise managers. When moving up in this stage, one has the benefit of extensive experience and knowledge, which can be applied to enrich the positions up the ladder.

A first time manager needs to be able to see this progression, and then devise a way to draw up something similar for the staff that are being managed. This will help to motivate them and reveal that there is a way they can get to the highest positions in the company.

Chapter 7:
Common Management Challenges and Solutions

Leaders and managers work in tough situations all the time. Managers for instance are required to manage people and the processes, both of which pose great challenges that managers have to go through at all times. Forming a team and seeing it through until it is able to realise the set goals is not a walk in the park. So many issues come up and a manager will find himself in tough situations that require proper decision making so as not to fail terribly in his role as a leader.

Many people do not see exactly how a management role can be challenging. This is because people tend to think that managers usually have the best time of their life, giving orders and supervising what has been done. What they do not know is that dealing with people who have hopes, fears and emotions is not very easy. People in a team have come from diverse backgrounds, therefore they are totally different and as a manager, you will be expected to work with them in the same team, for the same results.

Here are some management challenges that you can expect as you work with your team and how you can possibly deal with them:

1. When you know something important that affect some or all your team members but you are not allowed to share it with your team. A manager is the kind of person who is supposed to be open and close to his team. If you have been in management before, you probably have been facing situations where your team come to you with questions and you come out clean,

with all honesty. However, in some situations, this is not even possible. If for instance business has not been doing well and there is a possibility that some of the employees will be laid off from work, you will find it hard to tell that to the team that you have been working so closely with and maybe you are not required to share out such information. To be on the safe side, it is good to keep such information to yourself.

2. Risking losing an important employee because you have to enforce business policies. There are some employees that have the best intentions but they are always messing up and sometimes it becomes a great challenge for a manager to know what to do with them. Some of the mistakes they make are unforgivable and you are required to fire them at that instant. Because they are really good at what they do, even better than some of the other employees, you are not real sure if you have to enforce the policies at that instant or not. In such a situation, you have to do the right thing no matter how hard it seems. If you have evidence of his wrongdoing, it will only be right to let him go. This way, other employees will see that you mean business and that rules are applied fairly irrespective of how good a person is.

3. Not being able to reward a very talented employee in your team. As a manager, you will have that one person who is energetic, talented, always willing to take the challenges, one who is always helping others to finish their tasks and so on. Such employees always want to advance their careers and they also require other rewards, maybe a promotion or monetary benefits but you realize that you are in no position to offer that. The challenge here comes when you have no way to reward

him yet he is doing all he can to enter into your good books. Another challenge is that probably other employees are waiting to see just what you will do to snap at him. In such a situation, you can talk to that particular employee to explain what you can and what you cannot do but always make sure that you appreciate his efforts.

4. A situation which requires you to choose financial benefits over standards. A manager has a major responsibility not just to the organization that he is representing but also to the team he is working with. You are not only working for the goals of the organization but also to help your team acquire the right skills to be able to advance in their career. That is why every decision that you make, whether major or minor should be the best one because your team will be watching you closely to see what you are doing and this will shape them in the future. When you are faced with a tough situation that requires you to make a major decision, you have to discuss it with your team. Let them tell you what their view is pertaining to the issues at hand. Involving them will help them realize that some decisions have to be made not because it is the right thing to do but because it is necessary at that instant.

5. Handling conflicts in the office will always be a challenge especially conflicts that are not related to the business but they happen in the office. Do not expect that your employees will always get along. Some of them will create relationships that will go out of the office and when they fight out of office, such issues can affect the way that they work. An employee for instance can come to report mistreatment by another one and

through investigations, you realize that the root of the problem is not even work related. Sorting such interpersonal issues will be a challenge since you will have to be tough and the employee who will lose will always think that you were not fair. With such kind of issues, you have to be smart and only stick to the facts of the matter. You may be required to direct their communication at that instant in order to make it easier for them to work together in the team until they sort their issues outside the office.

Chapter 8:
Management Mistakes to
Watch out For

People are right when they say that making a mistake provides you with an opportunity to learn. However, sometimes some mistakes will live on however much you want to shake them off your shoulders. That is why it is good not to make the mistakes in the first place. When it comes to management, you should know that in management and leadership, there are people that are looking up on you for guidance, therefore a simple mistake may not go well with them. That is why it is good to know about some of the common mistakes one can make in leadership and management so as to be careful not to make them. This way, you can enjoy your success as a leader. Some of the most common mistakes leaders and managers make all the time are:

1. Not providing feedback

A manager should provide regular feedback just to ensure that things are working smoothly all the time. A single mistake should not be allowed to repeat itself if you do not want things to get out of hand as a manager; you need to handle such issues as soon as they are seen so as to move forward together as a team. Good leadership and management entails providing proper feedback on time and effectively, therefore if you will wait until the next time there will be a meeting in order to give a feedback, it might be too late.

2. Not defining goals beforehand

Goals should be set before a team starts working together. Goals are there to provide a clear guideline to what the team should work on and how they should work. Failing to define goals is a serious management mistake because the team will not know what they are working for and what they need to achieve by the end of each day. Goals should tell your team what they need to do and what they should achieve in the end, therefore they will have a good reason to work hard every day. With clear goals, they will know what they should do first, therefore the right goals will be achieved at the right time and this is what will define the success of a team.

3. Missing in action

Sometimes some projects are completed without the knowledge of a manager because he is hands off in so many things that happen in a team. What happens in such cases is that some projects will not be done right and this can cause so many problems for an organization or business. To avoid facing such an issue, you have to review the progress that your team makes so that the project will be properly done and completed. This way, you will save the frustration of having to deal with a wrong project and time too since your team will not have to repeat the entire project. This also helps you get closer to your team and this helps you to understand them better.

4. Too busy for your team

Other than leading a team, managers have other roles and responsibilities that they should take care of therefore not having enough time for his team is possible. A manager is also a human being, with his personal issues to handle. If you allow yourself to be too occupied with other things with little or no time for your team, you will fail terribly in your management agenda. You need to set some time aside for your team if you want to succeed in your management role. You can cancel some of your appointments for instance and meetings to be with your team. Also, you can stay connected to your team in such a manner that they can always come to you if they have a need or an issue that requires your attention.

5. Getting too close

Establishing close connection with your team is a good thing because this is the only way you will know them better to understand their strengths and weaknesses so that you can assign the right roles and responsibilities to them. However there is always a limit as to how close you can be with your team. You do not want to establish the kind of relationship who will make it hard for you to correct them in case the make a mistake. There has to be healthy boundaries between a manager and his team that will help them work closely and not really close to mess up with their working relationship.

6. Hiring in a hurry

Sometimes this happens especially if there is an urgent task that needs to be handled within a short period of time. Even if there is need to hire in a hurry, hiring in a hurry will be disastrous for a manger and the project can fail terribly. When there is so much to do and there is need to hire more people to work with your team, you have to do it soberly. You have to ensure that you are choosing the right people, not just anyone that comes your way and is in need of a job. There are effective recruitment tips that you can adopt even when you are in a hurry and they will help you get the right people in a short period of time. You have to avoid hiring the wrong people at all costs.

Conclusion

Being a first time manager may have been a scary thought when you first picked up the book. Once you get over the excitement of having the opportunity to make a difference, you are hit with self-doubt and fear and may wonder whether you would be able to make it as a manager.

This book has taught you that you are not alone with your concerns and that there is a solution you can find. This solution lies in being able to learn from the lessons of those who have been there before you, and to choose a management model that best suits the situation that you are facing.

This book contains a total of ten management models, each one meant to help you face something that is challenging in the work place. If you are unable to motivate your staff, you can seek the guidance of Maslow's hierarchy of needs to understand what could be holding them back. You can also use the changing phases by Kotter to understand change and cope with it in the best way possible.

Tuckman's stages of team development will help you to create an effective team who are able to achieve results without being micro-managed. This book has given you a practical answer to any concerns that you may have had about being a first time manger. Use it an improve your leadership and management skills immediately.

www.ingramcontent.com/pod-product-compliance
Lightning Source LLC
Chambersburg PA
CBHW071832200526
45169CB00018B/1416